Lorne B
FOREWORD B

UP
SHOTS

YOUTH ATHLETE RECRUITMENT GUIDE
the parent edition

SHOTS Up! Youth Athlete Recruitment Guide:
Parent Edition

Copyright © 2020 by Lorne Bowman, Sr.

ADEI Media Group
Southfield, MI 48075
contact@adeimedia.com
adeimedia.com

ISBN 13:   978-1-7358084-0-6

Printed in the United States of America. All rights reserved under International Copyright Law. Contents and/or cover may not be reproduced in whole or part in any form without the express written consent of the author, Lorne Bowman, Sr.

DEDICATION

First, I want to thank my Lord and Savior, Jesus Christ for giving me the inspiration to put my experiences into words. I would like to dedicate this book to my three beautiful children, Mariah, Lorne Jr., and Aaron who are my reasons why I get up to take it to the max every day.

Also, I'd like to dedicate this book to the entire Bowman family whom I love very much. To my Dad and Mom, Bishop Andrew, and Viveca Merritt, and the entire Merritt family.

To every coach and trainer that took the time to sow your gifts and talents into my son over the years. To all my basketball brotherhood of friends who been so supportive throughout this journey; and to all my friends and well-wishers.

May God bless you all.

Lorne Bowman, Sr.

FOREWORD

As parents, we all want the best for our children. Inherently, we want to shield them from the many perils that they will undoubtedly face. We want to achieve this through better educational systems, a safe and clean environment, and also competitive sports.

I included sports programs because many people are under the impression that sports are just that-sports. Many don't realize that sportsmanship actually, if done correctly, prepares us for life in more ways than imaginable. It really is a gateway to life by equipping children with many tools to be successful in whatever venture they set out to face. Basketball changed my life in so many ways and trust me, Dassie Coleman, certainly didn't have a blueprint. It not only allowed me to connect with people all over the world, but it also prepared me in closing major business deals.

With the advent of social media platforms, the kids are being evaluated completely different. We are all familiar with the African proverb "It takes a village to raise a child."

Shots Up! is an extraordinary extension of the "village" as it gives insightful tools to help train our children in the way they should go (Proverbs 22:6)!

Derrick Coleman
NBA 1st overall draft pick [1990]
NBA Rookie of the Year [1991]
NBA All-Star [1994]

INTRODUCING SHOTS UP!

Are you in or are you out? Let's start right there. Before you take your child any further down this path of athletics and game play, you, as the parent, will need to answer this question for yourself.

I've been there. As I write this book, my son, Lorne Jr. will be leaving home to further his journey at the University of Wisconsin-Madison. To be honest, I wish I had known more in the beginning. Before my son started down this path, I wish I had a book, a resource, a coach, or a friend to help me understand some of the things that I am about to share with you.

Yes, we learned together. We prayed together. We moved forward and navigated through this process together with God as our guide. There was no way that I wanted to have all this knowledge, experience, and understanding and not share it with other parents to equip them to be in a better position than I was to help their children succeed and go to the next level, no matter which path they choose to take.

SEASONS

Life is about seasons. The older I get, the more I understand this fundamental truth. We have some areas of life where seasons come around again and again. Yet there are others that don't come around as often, if ever in a lifetime. However, what I do know is that every season has a purpose. It's with that understanding that we must help our children navigate their growth as human beings and as athletes who desire to move down the path of game play at the next level.

You will find this book has been divided into three sections. Let me explain them below.

Pre-Season or Training Camp

In this section, we will discuss what happens before the recruiting phase starts. We delve into

- How to identify, handle, and groom a child that shows a skill set for the game early on.
- Important factors necessary when you have other children who are not athletic in the home.
- Setting boundaries and creating internal contracts.
- Cultivating mindset and building character.

All these critical elements have either been witnessed or experienced during my journey with athletes and can help, hinder or blindside your child's chances for advancement in the recruitment stage. Training camp or pre-season as it is, also offers some tremendous benefits and opportunities nestled in this time that should not be overlooked or taken for granted.

Recruitment or Regular Season

Make no mistake. Recruitment is a season!

There is so much preparation, politics, and process that goes into the behind-the-scenes of not only getting your child ready for next level play, if that is the path that they are going to take; but of other considerations that may have never crossed your mind. Even the small things that seem innocent on the outside can be landmines if you don't know how to navigate the terrain properly.

Getting through recruitment is going to be where the most intensity and discipline can be found of all the seasons. Unlike training camp, everything counts in this season and for some, it can be stressful and completely overwhelming. Just remember, *Shots Up!* was written to navigate the muddy waters of recruitment with you in my thoughts.

I want you to keep one major thing in mind during the regular season. You and your child are partners to get them to the next level and the best thing that you can do is calm down and make the best decision, play-by-play.

You can and will make it through this time with success as your goal by staying focused, listening to your coach, trusting your teammates, and working with the end in mind. Parents, when you do this, not only will you become the example of what it takes during their next season of play, I believe that you and your child will reap a caveat of rewards along the next stages and phases of their future life paths.

Post-Season or 'Select and Sign'

You made it to the post-season! Now we get to talk about reaping some of the rewards and reviewing the playbook that we used to get to this point.

You guys have left it all on the court; but you can't celebrate too hard or too long at this stage. There are some additional key takeaways that can position you for their college career if you are mindful of them early in this season.

That's what this is all about, right? Setting your child on the path to achieve success at every level. I know that is what motivates me when it comes to my children. I want them to experience success on every level and in every season of life. That's where my heart and desire come into writing this book. Yes, *Shots Up!* is about recruitment, but it's also about even more than that. It's about relationships. The relationship that you have with your child; the relationship your child has with the game, the process, and the purpose. Which will ultimately transcend game play and help create a mindset that builds character perseverance, and their relationships with others throughout their lifetime—no matter where they find themselves, on or off the court.

SECTION ONE
PRE-SEASON PREPARATION

"My son shot the ball and kept his hand extended with great form after that release." (Hmm)

I had taken him to Dave and Busters, where he played the 'pop-a-shot machine' where you shoot the basketball in the net to land a prize. It was my first mental note of his potential.

He was 2.

As he got older, I noticed that he had a genuine interest in the game, which over time continued to increase. Then came bigger and taller rims with near perfect form, extension, and follow-through.

He was only 4 or 5 by then.

By the time my son was six years old, I had already taken the initiative to see if this was something that he might really want to take more seriously. Parents at this point, please take note that I was placing him in situations that gave him opportunities to play the game. I was not running out, calling coaches, or pushing him to play. As a parent, I had to keep focused on my son and make sure that I was watching him very closely and staying aware of his interest level, not just his skill set.

I did things like enroll him in remedial basketball training at the local recreation center. Where after a couple years, I realized that my son, Lorne Jr., did have something very special athletically inside of him. Keep in mind, I still had to be careful how I handled the talent and ability that was in him.

At the point where I believed that he was enjoying basketball and had a skill set for the game, I went and signed him up for an organized basketball league. I didn't just sign him up for the closest and most convenient league to my home. I understood that in order for him to get better, he needed to be challenged. This is true for anyone and everything in life. I knew that the right league for my son was a league where the kids were just as good, if not better than he was.

He needed the battle scars, the tough games, the losses, and defeats. I wanted him to fight for rebounds against guys that were twice his size. He wouldn't be the best scorer if he couldn't put up the numbers against some of the best scorers and play makers in the state.

Yes, parents, it was hard to watch some days. After all, that's my son out there on that court. That's your son and daughter out in the middle of what becomes an all out battle during some games. It's not always fun to grow and develop in order to make it to the next level, but it's necessary to test the talent. Take them to the limit and then see if your child has what it takes to succeed in this game or not.

As parents, our children are taking us on a journey to their greatness with them. Our job is to steer, guide, and encourage them at every step of the way. Some of the decisions in our part of the process are harder at times than others. As was the case with Lorne Jr., but I knew it had to be this way if my son were going to be the best athlete and basketball player that he could be.

As time went on Lorne Jr. got better and stronger. I knew he had the talent and skill set to play the game that he loved. So not only was there going to be more sacrifice for him, but even more sacrifice was going to be required of me too. The next phase of his basketball journey was going to require him playing for an exceptional travel organization. They are known for developing kids by playing the toughest teams in and out of the state.

Parents of course I am proud of my son and his accomplishments, but please know that there is more to getting into the athletics journey than the athletes, skills, and games themselves. I would like you to consider that one of the biggest aspects of this journey may be the most unspoken one of all.

THE CONTRACT

There is a certain point in this journey with your child that grows larger than how many points your child scored or who has bragging rights, especially when you start investing more financial commitment, time, and sacrifice; you both are going to start having goals. Listen to me, the contract or the scholarship is going to become the goal if you keep at this long enough.

Which is why when we arrived at this stage, I saw this as an opportunity to instill the importance of honor, integrity, and character. Also, my son had to realize the potential consequences of signing a contract and not upholding his end of the agreement. He had to understand how it could potentially impact his future.

I believe these lessons are better learned with you, as a parent, than with a basketball team or coach who doesn't have the same emotional attachment or responsibility for your child as you do as their parent.

Hence, I wanted to be the first person that my son signed a contract with. So, at the point that I knew that the best fit for him was joining this travel league, I sat down and had a discussion with him.

I talked to him about what my expectations were of him and what he could expect from me. We drafted a contract with each other that was simple and straightforward, outlining our promises to one another.

He promised to keep his grades high; turn in all his homework assignments on time; and finally, he promised that every time he stepped on the court, whether for a practice or a game, that he would give it everything he had.

If he did all of those things, I promised, I would support him no matter where this journey took him, down to my last dollar. And I am extremely grateful to say that he has been a man of his word, keeping the promises that he made to me that day.

Some of you might be wondering would I potentially stop my son's advancement to the next level because of his academics? What would I have done if his grades dropped, while he was excelling on the basketball court? Would I have pulled the plug on him playing the game that he loved?

My answer is without hesitation, "Yes!"

We never know what life is going to bring our way, do we? Your child might not know that, but you do. As parents, we know that things don't always work out as planned.

I don't want my son limited to one opportunity. I want him to have the option to choose his path, not have to settle for what's left over if one thing doesn't materialize the way he had hoped.

There are those who don't agree with me, but I believe as a parent in the journey with a young athlete, academics must be a prerequisite for athletic participation.

My motto has always been this, "Hard work in the classroom and on the field."

We will have greater success when we set the boundaries and expectations around our children that way.

CHARACTER

Student athletics is extremely competitive and can be a slippery slope when it comes to being character driven. The contract with my son was an exercise of his character as much as it was about anything else.

Colleges are looking for athletes with character now more than ever. Listen to me when I tell you that all the recent rash of incidents on college campuses and the less than honorable character decisions that some professional athletes have made in the past, have oftentimes cost universities and sports franchises more than the athlete was worth in scholarships and ticket sales.

Part of the recruitment process is about your child's character. Who they are off the court is just as important as what they do on the court. I have personally witnessed youth athletes, both male and female, get passed over for recruitment because of character issues off the court even when they had stellar play on it.

I bring this up in the "Pre-Season" because this is something that you must keep before your child at the very beginning.

Character is one of those keys that doesn't seem like much until you can't open the door to opportunity without it.

Let's say that you've built your home the way that you always dreamed. It's furnished the way you like. Now I want you to reflect on the amount of time and energy that you put into making it a perfect environment for you and your family. You have the culture and comfort that you all enjoy. Wouldn't it be difficult or nearly impossible for you to invite someone who is disruptive and seems to bring trouble wherever they go to live in your house for four years?

Of course it would! That's the impact of character from the perspective of a college or university that starts scouting players for their school.

That's what character means to the college and universities that will be recruiting your child at the next level. I can't stress this point enough. Character is a crucial aspect of next level success.

ONE SHOT

For the most part, it becomes evident rather early that a child has the talent and desire to play sports. From the time they start, until their *Letter of Intent*, to the college they choose; you and your child are only going to have one shot to get this right.

I know it doesn't sound fair, but many times, life isn't fair. With this, there is no room for error. Your child has ten other student athletes that are just as good as they are waiting on him or her to make a mistake, so they can take their place.

We both know that not only is recruitment a process, it starts long before we even know that they are looking at our children.

Someone is keeping a file from the moment they play their first game.

Carelessness on social media for instance is a cruel way to lose your shot because you and your child didn't understand that everything they post, you post, and the friends and family that you both are connected to are being interviewed too.

Don't allow the silliness of something as simple as social media sabotage the shot that you are working so hard to get. Always remind your child often to get and keep a clean image. Stay away from controversy and stay focused on the things that are most important. Landing a scholarship or another opportunity might open up because of their focus, perseverance, and determination.

It's all about the goal ahead for him or her, and not the many distractions that threaten to derail their progress, or stifle the options that are on the road ahead of them.

You've made too many sacrifices to allow self-inflicted wounds and poor decisions to have the last say. Like I said, "one shot." Make sure to guard it wisely.

EXPOSURE

At the point that your kid is good enough to earn a scholarship offer, it's very important to guide them down the right path to get noticed. Exposure for your child doesn't always come to your doorstep. In most cases you must take the initiative to make things happen for them.

There are different ways to get your child noticed. Some good and others not so much. This is why it's important that you know the most effective ways to exhibit your athletes' skill set.

Let's take a closer look.

AAU: Just because you have your child playing on an AAU (Amateur Athletic Union) team doesn't mean that your kid is getting the exposure necessary to get the proper looks that they need. There are a lot of AAU teams that play travel sports. However, to get noticed you'll need to choose an organization that can place him or her in the best position to be seen.

You need to understand where college coaches go to recruit kids. Typically, they are going to gravitate towards the organizations that play the toughest competition.

Although there are other areas of AAU play that your child can receive exposure, in my experience these four circuits are the most popular.

- The EYBL (Elite Youth Basketball League)
- Adidas Gauntlet
- Under Armour
- NY2LA (New York To Los Angeles)

These circuits attract hundreds of college coaches. Knowing this try to get your child placed on a team that's affiliated with one of the above circuits. This will increase their chances of being seen by coaches who are looking for recruits.

High School: In addition to AAU, playing on the high school basketball team can be a good place to gain exposure as well. It's important to know that there are two things that are significant as it relates to getting noticed at the high school level.

- The athlete must be good enough to attract college coaches to come and watch them at the high school level.
- He or she is playing with someone who's good enough to attract college coaches.

Every year there's a period during the high school season where college coaches can come to a high school and watch the students play. This is called "The Open Period." It's during this time where kids get an opportunity to showcase their skills in front of colleges who are looking to add talent to their rosters.

I remember during an "Open Period" when several coaches came to watch my son play. I recall a coach telling me that they also liked several other kids on the team who they originally had not come to see.

It was exciting to think that my son's teammates were getting attention from college coaches that they might not have even expected.

The goal is getting your child in front of coaches. It doesn't matter who the coach came to see. What matters is that your child is there, doing their best every game, every touch, every play.

Let me stop here and interject an important note about high school.

Where my son went to high school was also part of the pre-season stage of his journey. It was important to have him in a school that had a solid academic foundation. We also looked for a high school that he could continue to develop his athletic ability.

His high school played a tremendous role in keeping him focused; educationally and athletically. My family is forever grateful for the years of support that his high school afforded him during his time there.

Keep this in mind when it comes to selecting the high school that your child attends. Even if it means going out of the district or area that you currently reside to increase their chances for academic and athletic excellence. I believe it is something to consider.

It's important to know how these things work at the high school level so your child will have something to work towards. When those college coaches show up, he or she is ready. Again, the point here is to just get your kid anywhere where the lights are shining and he or she can get noticed.

Recruiting Services: There are a lot of people out there who will tell you that they can do this, or they can do that. Every parent wants their child to get a scholarship opportunity. But you've got to be cautious of *recruiting services* who promise a lot and charge a ton. I'm not saying that all recruiting services are bad. But what I am saying is to do your research and know exactly what you're getting into before you give anybody your money who's making it sound easy to get your child a scholarship offer.

In my opinion the most solid way for a kid to get a scholarship is going to come from hard work and dedication. If it's meant to be, it is going to be the hard work that will eventually put you in a position to develop the relationships with college coaches who may eventually offer your child a scholarship. In my experience if it sounds too good to be true, it probably is. Especially, if the recruiting service is not focused on your child maintaining grades, integrity, and putting in hard work all the way. I was always told growing up that when you have the goods, you don't have to say a word. There will be a path beaten to your doorstep. In other words, put in the work and don't stop because the cream will always rise to the top.

Camps: During the summer there will be a lot of camps being held, some camps are by invitation only and others require a fee to attend. There are also colleges who hold camps to observe talent for potential scholarship opportunities. These camps more than likely will be by invitation only.

What I like about camps is they can be a good source of exposure. However, knowing which camps are worth investing your child's time and effort is important. You must do your research when deciding where to go. In my opinion, it's ok to pay for a camp if the camp is being run by the coaching staff of an actual team. At least you want your child seen by the decision makers, and at that point it'll be up to him or her to showcase their talents to the level of being noticed.

If you're being invited to a camp, more than likely, this means that your child has already turned some heads and he or she is being considered as someone who has potential. If a college specifically invites you to one of their camps, it's a good idea to go. They no doubt have already heard about your child and want to take a further look at their skills up close.

My son, Lorne Jr., was invited to multiple camps but the one that stood out to me was from the University of Wisconsin.

When the camp started, I noticed that the head coach and all the assistant coaches were running every aspect of the camp. They were taking notes and paying close attention to each player. It was obvious that they were on a mission to find the best talent. This is what you should be looking for in a camp. My son was in front of the people who can make the decision necessary to determine if an offer would be made. That's all we can ask for as a parent.

SECTION TWO
REGULAR SEASON RECRUITMENT

Out the gate, I want to tell you to relax and take a deep breath. For most families, this is at least a four-year process. Settle your nerves and gather yourself. The other thing I want to let you know as we go through this recruiting process is that you are not alone. That's right. You heard me correctly, you are <u>not</u> alone.

One of the benefits of going through this process is all the wonderful people that you are going to meet along the way. Of course, this is a competitive sport, but everyone is out there for the same reason. Supporting their child's aspirations for success.

Most of the people you meet will be cheering just as loud for your child as they are for their own. You become a family with a common goal in mind, winning games, and having a successful outcome—seeing your children get to the next level of play. You know that those young people have been hanging around your house and riding in your car all this time. There is no way that those friendship bonds are going to be broken that easily. Honestly, I believe they get tighter the further we get into the recruitment process.

PROTECT YOUR CHILD

I was always taught that the best thing you can do when entering into anything is to get a good understanding and gather all the information that you can about what you are about to get involved in.

Not only have I come to understand the great wisdom in this advice, but it has helped me look at everything I do with a desire to know as much as I can about any given situation. Believe me, this one piece of advice has saved me from a whole lot of missteps along the way on multiple occasions.

Parents and guardians, please go into this understanding that the business of recruiting is a two-way street. On one side of the street is the college or university standing there with shiny trinkets and an abundance of opportunities sitting there for the taking.

Let me back up and say that again! RECRUITING IS A BUSINESS. It is our job to protect our children as they go down the recruitment path.

The school is driving the recruiting engine and it is very easy to get swept up in the excitement of seeing your child placed in this incredibly favorable position. CAUTION: Grab hold of your emotions and remember that it's your child standing on the other side of the street. You are going to have to be their protector by exercising common sense and emotional control even when you are jumping up and down inside screaming, "That's my child up there!" In the tantum of your excitement, keep in mind that your kid is putting in the work to get to this stage of play.

Let's review a couple crucial facts that will help keep you grounded when the reflection of those shiny trinkets begin to sparkle.

The life blood of any school's athletic program is recruiting kids. Everyone wants to win and the only way that happens is if the college program gets the best talent they can. Take that knowledge just a bit further by unpacking exactly what that means.

It means that your child has value. The school is going to increase revenue by ticket sales, products, and alumni when they bolster a winning record. Yes, your child's education is being paid for by the school, but the child is increasing the profitability of the school as well.

Think of it this way. Your child is partnering with the school that they choose when it comes time to sign a *Letter of Intent* if it gets to that point.

I have witnessed lots of parents get so excited about their child being recruited, but make sure that the decision and offer on the table doesn't adversely affect the kid's future two or three years in.

Yes, you want the scholarship money and all the other opportunities afforded them. But you also want your child in a safe environment with faculty and staff that are going to be as diligent and committed to your child's education and future success as you are.

BE ON GUARD

One day I noticed a call coming into my phone from a number that I didn't recognize. When I picked up the call there was a man on the other end who identified himself as someone who worked for a sports agent.

His words to me were, "We've been watching your son for a while now and have identified him as a pro ball player. We've helped other pros in the past get shoe contracts with the NBA and we'd like to meet with you at our office."

Now keep in mind, my son was only a seventeen-year-old junior in high school at the time. I immediately told him that I'm not interested in anything like that, because my son needs to focus on his grades and choosing a school for college.

I shared that story to explain how soon you must be on guard from those who will try and derail your child for their own benefit. I understood that they were not calling me for my son's benefit. It wasn't about my son at all, it was about them.

If I had let my guard down and met with them and let them pay for dinner or I took a gift from them to give my son on their behalf, I would've violated NCAA rules which could have destroyed his scholarship opportunities later on. (We will talk about the NCAA recruiting rules later).

Everybody is not your friend, and these people (who you don't know) are not in your corner. It's up to us as parents to educate ourselves and our children about what to do and what not to do during the recruiting process. Sharks lurk in deep water with promises of gifts, money, fame, etc. Our kids are easily accessible through social media and that's where the people who want to get close to them will go to approach them. They know that the parents aren't around, and they'll move in and try to latch themselves on them in a stealth, underhanded type of way.

I recall having to call one coach in particular that contacted my son through Twitter when he was a freshman (fourteen years old) in high school asking him a ton of questions that should have been directed to me. I politely asked him not to reach out to my son again, but he was welcome to call me if he had any other questions regarding my son.

Listen, you can't let your guard down, not even for a second. Always be in the room with your kids even though you might not be doing the talking. In other words, don't allow your child's training or regular season process get too far away from you. You should always have your finger on the pulse of what's going on during the journey.

Keep your guard up and your feet steady.

You must think about these things at the beginning of the recruitment process. Not at the point when things start heating up and the excitement and pride over your child's accomplishments are washing over you. I strongly encourage you to remember that a partnership is a two-way street--a win-win for both parties involved.

KEEP YOUR EYE ON THE PRIZE

There are many moving components to the recruiting process, but there is one thing that must stay at the forefront of your mind and that is the ultimate goal. With age will come many challenges, things that will come along that can put your child in a precarious position that if not handled correctly can result in major setbacks, if not totally detailing them from achieving their dreams. It is important to understand how critical it is to continue to express to our children the importance of staying on the right track and keeping their eye on the prize. I was always taught, and have in turn taught my children, that if it doesn't feel right then remove yourself from the situation; and if it doesn't look right then don't partake in it at all. Trust your instincts and don't override what you know to be the right thing to do. I teach my children that there is NO right way to do wrong and to shun the very appearance of evil. It is inevitable that our children will come across compromising situations whether with the opposite sex, hanging around the wrong crowd, or anything that could be a distraction to the plan set before them. Remember one wrong decision can set you back tremendously, if not totally destroy everything you've worked so hard for. Be smart, stay focused and keep to the plan.

Let me share a story about the farmer and the horse. One day there was a horse, who was grazing in the field. He stumbled and fell into a very large hole in the ground. When the farmer saw what happened, he determined that the hole was too big to get the horse out of so he wrote the horse off as a lost cause. The farmer decided the only thing to do was to bury the horse right where he stood, however the horse had other plans. The farmer began to shovel dirt on the horse, but the horse made up his mind that he was gonna keep his eye on the prize which was to get out of that hole.

Therefore, every time the farmer would throw dirt on the horse, the horse would shake it off and pack it under his feet. The farmer continued to throw dirt but the horse stuck to his plan of shaking it off and packing it under his feet. After a while, something remarkable began to happen and the horse's plan began to work. After hours of shaking off the dirt and packing it under his feet, the horse began to rise out of the hole. Then finally with one last shake and one last pack, he was able to jump out of the hole to safety. The situation that was meant for the horse's doom was turned around for his victory because he devised a plan and kept his eye on the prize. The moral of the story is to not allow anything to knock you off your square. Don't allow anybody to dictate your outcome; when you make your plan, stick with it, follow it through, stay on guard and I promise just like that horse, your plan will be fulfilled also.

LEARN WHAT YOU DON'T KNOW

Remember the advice, "Get a good understanding and gather all the information that you can about what you are about to get involved with." I'm bringing that to your attention again because the old saying is true. "What you don't know can hurt you." In this case our children.

That's why I think it's important to arm yourself with as much information as you possibly can to truly protect the best interest of your child.

Every parent whose child plays sports would love for them to receive a college scholarship. It is a gratifying feeling knowing that after all the years of hard work that someone has taken notice to the point of putting a scholarship offer on the table. I can recall when my son received his first offer from the University of Buffalo. I literally cried tears of joy because I was so happy and proud of him. Since then I have learned a lot as it relates to scholarship offers from both a parent and the school's perspective. Let me tell you that both are vital to understand as you go down this path. First, you need to understand what a scholarship offer means. When a school extends an offer to an athlete, at that moment they've concluded he or she is someone that can help their team win. However, you also need to understand that an offer is just a verbal communication and that things can change as time moves on. Sometimes, time can change in the opposite direction if you, as the parent, are not careful.

In other words, just because you get a verbal offer doesn't mean that it's etched in stone. There are several reasons why things can change, including but not limited to injury; lower academic performance; behavior issues; or that which very few parents consider-- simply waiting too long to accept an offer.

Waiting Too Long to Accept An Offer

You need to educate yourself on how many scholarships the school has remaining when the offer is extended to your child.

Find out how many other kids they extended offers to as well. This is important because if you have a strong interest in attending that school, in my opinion, it will be in your best interest not to wait to see what else may or may not come through.
There's an old saying, "A bird in the hand is better than two in the bush."

By taking the time to look at things from the school's perspective, these coaches have been charged with building their athletic programs. Although your child is talented, I hate to be the one to tell you but there are lots of talented kids out there. When your child is targeted as someone they want, time is of the essence. The longer you allow the offer to sit on the table, the more it reduces the chances of you being a part of that program.

I have a lot of friends who have children that went through and are going through their recruiting journey. One situation stands out to me that I believe is worth mentioning to illustrate this point.

A good buddy of mine has a son that did extremely well in his sport while in high school. He excelled and was considered one of the best players in the state as a senior. He had racked up fifteen scholarship offers during his junior and senior years, but when it came time to commit to one of those fifteen schools, only five were left on the table. Why did this happen?

Universities don't always wait on the kid to make up their mind, but instead they move on to the next kid. I've said this before, recruiting is a two-way street and if there's not much coming back from your side of the street, a school can assume that you may not be as interested in their offer. Again, they will move on to another kid who they believe they have a better chance of signing.

You must understand that there are more athletes than scholarships and schools do not like it when kids sit on their offers. They can afford to move on so the real question becomes, can you afford to wait? I was once told by an assistant coach of a major program that if parents would educate themselves on how the process works it would make things a lot easier on their children, thus putting their child in a much better position overall.

As a parent, educating yourself is a vital component of the successful outcome for your child. I commend you for picking up this book, because it means that you understand that there are things that you don't know. Like I said before, I have been where you are. And am grateful that at this stage, I can say that my son is happy with the school and academic program that he is now a part of, with a full athletic scholarship to a Division I school.

I did what I could to educate myself through every part of the journey. You need to know how to maneuver through the process so if any critical decisions need to be made, you'll know what to do. Looking back a few years ago, there was a kid who was extremely talented, very athletic, and stood about 6 feet 6 inches tall. I had seen him play before and was absolutely convinced that he was Division I material beyond a shadow of a doubt. However, he went to a school in a part of the state that didn't get much exposure when he played.

One day I saw him play and met his parents. After talking to them I could tell that they were very green and didn't know much about the recruiting process. They didn't understand that they needed to get him in a space where he could get more exposure so that he could maximize his chances of getting the best possible scholarship opportunity that would be in line with his athletic talent. As a result, this kid ended up under achieving, in my opinion, and settling for a Division II school that was much smaller than what his talents should have afforded him.

You can't expect your child to know all the ins and outs of the recruiting process. I can't say this enough, parents need to be in the trenches helping navigate through what can be an overwhelming experience; and educating ourselves is the only way we can be everything we need to be for them during this time.

At the end of the day it's not about seeing how many offers you can stack up. The only thing that does is bolster your ego. Until your child commits to a school and signs a national *Letter of Intent* to attend that school, an offer is just verbal communication and nothing more.

UNDERSTANDING DIVISIONS

What are Divisions?

The NCAA Intercollegiate sports are categorized into three divisions.

DIVISION I

Division I schools have:

- The largest student bodies
- The largest athletic budgets
- The highest and most athletic scholarships
- The best athletic facilities

DIVISION II

Division II schools have:

- Smaller student bodies
- Smaller athletic departments and budgets
- Full athletic scholarships are rare (more partial scholarships awarded)

DIVISION III

Division III schools have:

- No athletic scholarships offered
- Most students receive need-based aid
- Less focus on the athletic department

Why is it important to know the differences between divisions? You need to know what your child's options are when it comes to their athletic career; not all athletic departments are created equal.

Now, let's look at the NCAA and the recruitment calendar that is designed to protect your child and regulate the recruiting process as a whole.

Let's talk about the most prominent governing body of intercollegiate sports athletics, the National Collegiate Athletic Association (NCAA). Many of the college sporting events that are televised like March Madness are competitions within the NCAA. The NCAA was established in part to promote a fair recruiting process and limit the disruptive behavior to the student and their families.

As a parent one of the reasons it is imperative that you become familiar with who the NCAA is and what their role is in collegiate sports is because not only do they have prominence in Divisional Leagues, but part of their responsibility is to enforce the rules established within its membership of colleges and universities athletic programs. They oversee everything, from financial aid and scholarships to recruiting and eligibility guidelines.

For the purposes of this book, I will be focusing on the Division I guidelines because Division I teams offer the highest scholarship awards and have the most competitive athletic programs. Most students and their parents aspire to be recruited by this division.

However, again I say, parents must educate themselves!

What Time Is It?

In recruiting there is a timeline or calendar for everything. The NCAA rules and guidelines are based on a recruiting calendar and every action within that process has a window of opportunity attached to it.

If you child is as serious about taking their sports journey to the next level, I am sure they have this calendar memorized. If you are anything like me, I wanted to make sure that I have a concrete understanding of timelines that coincide with all the other children in my home, and activities that being an adult requires.

I suggest you add these dates to your family calendar or create a separate calendar in a designated place just for these recruiting milestones.

It's important to note that the recruiting timetable starts in the middle of your child's junior year. I don't believe it's ever too soon to start educating yourself and preparing your family for all the activities that may lay ahead of you.

Recruitment is not a single person endeavor. It involves or should involve the entire family. I'll delve into this more in detail later. I know that the recruitment stage can seem difficult to deal with but don't get disheartened, there is something good at the end of all of this for your child. I truly believe that!

January—March

During this season, I don't want you or your child to get in the way of opportunity, simply by not evaluating as many variables as you can. Although I mentioned this idea of behavior and character before, I think it bears reviewing again at this stage.

Don't Get in the Way

When the time comes for the recruiting process to start, it's important to remember that although colleges may be looking at your child, they are looking at you too! What you say or do can and will affect them as well. You must look at yourself as a silent partner in the arrangement.

Let's say you were dating someone who has children and you want to get married, although you're marrying your partner the children are coming along with the deal as well. Colleges understand going into the process that they are not just getting the kid, but they are getting you too. It's very important that you support your child through his or her process from a reachable distance. How we carry ourselves speaks volumes. I recall when my son's recruiting started to heat up. I started receiving Facebook friend requests from different coaches who were looking at my son. I asked myself, if these schools are recruiting my son then why are they looking at my Facebook page?

Well it became evident that they wanted to see the type of person I was too. They were doing their homework to see if the parent of the kid that they are recruiting has any questionable character issues, or any potential red flags that they needed to know about. I had to check myself. I went through all my social media to make sure that I didn't post anything that could hurt my son. I have been on this journey with him for fifteen years. I've seen the struggles; I've lived the ups and downs; and I was there for every injury. I had to console him after heartbreaking losses. I was there to witness the countless hours of training; the thousands of shots he's taken in practice; in addition, we've traveled on many road trips and he's played game after game.

He's put in literal blood, sweat, and tears; and there is absolutely no way that I was going to do anything to get in the way of what he had worked so hard to accomplish. If you think for a second that your character and image as a parent doesn't mean anything then you're sadly mistaken.

I remember speaking to a coach of a major program. He shared with me that there had been disappointment several times while recruiting kids that their program was very interested in. He mentioned traveling to watch the prospect play but walked away very disappointed at how the kid's parents behaved during the game. Because of this, they backed off the prospect completely.

He stated that they didn't want to take a chance on bringing in that kid because the parents would have to come too. Now because of no fault of his or her own, the kid lost out on that scholarship opportunity because of their parents.

Just as good as your kid is on the field of play, we must match our image as parents during their recruiting process. A kid can make one poor decision that can ruin their chance at a scholarship. Likewise, as parents, we can do the same thing by how we conduct ourselves.

Please keep that in mind as you are taking this time to pull things together to start the recruiting journey. As always, your child has a part to play and you have one too. Play your role with wisdom and discretion. It will go a long way in the end; I promise you that!

One other important thing to note is that this is a great time to start a list of all the things that your child would like to get out of his or her college experience. Encourage them to think outside of their athletic aspirations and look at the interests they have beyond the sport.

I did this exercise with my son at the beginning of recruitment. I wanted him to take advantage of everything that his college experience had to offer beyond athletics.

Should your child have a desire for business, medicine, or engineering? Schools that are strong in those areas, academically, should be on the short list criteria when selecting a school, in case they have a recruitment possibility later down the line. Do this now.

I can assure you that when recruitment starts to heat up, they will not have the time or the energy to think with the end in mind. Believe me, now is the time to take advantage of this uninterrupted clarity.

March—May

We talked about this earlier, but these are the months that you should be reaching out to coaches, and letting them know that your kid is interested in their athletic program (if necessary).

Remind yourselves that coaches will not always know that a prospect exists. You may have to do some work to put your child in the best possible position, by visiting schools on their short list. Scheduling unofficial visits is a great way to make this happen.

Your kid has put in a whole lot to get here. They have been on their grind this whole time. You can't afford not to match their level of effort.

As you start fast forwarding through his or her recruiting process, you must understand what's coming over the horizon. There is going to be a level of commitment from you that is going to push you beyond your own limits and desires. This is the support that your child is going to need.

Depending on the intensity that your child is being recruited will determine just how much of a grind it will be for you as the parents. If you know early that your child is talented and will probably be pursued by colleges for a potential scholarship opportunity, then it makes sense to start preparing long before their junior year in high school.

By the time your child is on a school's radar, he or she may be asked to participate in different camps over the summer that colleges host to take a better look at potential athletes.

It's to your advantage if at all possible, to attend as many camps (that you're invited to) as you can during the recruiting period. This is a great way for your child to showcase his or her skills in front of the entire coaching staff. Keep in mind that they extended your student athlete an invitation for a reason.

The GRIND

I mentioned the grind before. Since it will be your responsibility to get your kid to and from each camp, meeting, and or event.

There may be multiple opportunities at different schools, in different states, at the same time. However, in order to put your child in front of as many eyes as possible, it becomes a necessary grind.

I recall during Lorne Jr.'s journey when he was invited to multiple camps and multiple unofficial visits in several states.

Although I didn't know what the outcome would be, I knew it was in my son's best interest to get him to each one. I had to figure out a way to pull this off between my work schedule and all the travel that was involved.

However, once I mapped out our travel itinerary, we hit the road. We flew to Wisconsin to participate in their camp that they had invited him to. Then, we drove to Purdue to do the same. I remember driving my son to Iowa for an unofficial visit, where there were no promises of a scholarship at all. I knew it was my job to get him there.

The drive was eight hours one way and I'm not one for driving long distances. It was a brutal drive for me. There were times I felt sleepy on the road and I had to pull over, but I kept going.

There were times that I felt like we were going all the way to this college or that university with no guarantee in sight, just an invitation.

I knew in my heart what I didn't know in my head sometimes. If I didn't get him there, nothing would happen for my son, but if I kept grinding, even though I didn't feel like I had the strength to do it all some days, I would press forward anyways. For my children—I would do anything to help them be successful.

After we arrived at the University of Iowa, we were met by the assistant coach who was recruiting my son. Shortly after that we were taken into the head coach's office where he offered my son a full basketball scholarship to play for the University of Iowa. I was thrilled.

Let's say I made the trip about me. Since I didn't like long drives, say I decided not to go at all, even though my son had worked hard enough to earn a full scholarship. Things may have turned out differently for him. The scholarship offer may have never happened because I wasn't willing to grind it out for him.

I realized a very important lesson that day. That the grind isn't about me (the parent), it is about my son (the child) and that's all that matters.

Not only that, we drove to Valparaiso for an unofficial visit and although the University of Michigan and Michigan State University were a lot closer, I had to make the time to get him there, as well. It was a sacrifice, but it was necessary.

As parents, we should see these things from the perspective that it's a part of the program. It's what we do as parents to make sure that we put our children in the absolute best position to win. Get yourself prepared both mentally, physically, and financially because it's coming, and the better prepared you are, the easier the grind will be.

Also, keep in mind that we were still looking and taking advantage of every opportunity. Yes, we ended up with multiple offers, but that's because we wanted to examine each school that my son wanted to consider. I advise you and your child to do the same. Keep looking for a school that best fits your child. There is nothing wrong with contacting coaches and highlighting your child's athletic ability during your prospecting along the way.

April—August

The only thing that your child should be thinking about during this time is playing well. Afterall, you both presumably have done the work and made the financial commitment to visit schools and contact athletic departments, vying for the attention of the coaching staff.

Don't do all that work and then NOT give the coaches what they are looking for, which is a showcase of their skills, sportsmanship, and potential. Remind them to play every game in a way that says, "I'm the student that you want playing for your team!" Your child must have the mindset to figure out what's going to cause them to stand out among the rest of the recruits. As a parent, have the mindset that the school is giving something, but they are getting something too--a great student with great athletic ability.

August—November

Up to this point, we have been throwing a broad net, reeling in whatever jumped on the hook. Now the time has come to start narrowing down the serious prospects. Which schools are really showing an interest? Do those schools have an academic program that is going to align with their educational goals that your child has for themselves?

Laser focus on what the goal is beyond the four years and remove athletics out of the equation. Plan for the next ten years, not just the next four. This exercise is made popular by many CEOs of major corporations and government leaders. What is the ten-year plan? This is going to help steer the four-year selection in a big way!

Parents we can't do this for them though. We can want to make decisions for our children at this stage, but we can't. As hard as it will be for you, they will need to spur this decision from their own heart.

Of course, we will be there to assist, guide, and support, but we must give them the freedom to review their options and choose the best one for themselves. Let me say again how hard this can be. We cannot interfere, and decide for our child. At this stage, we can only encourage. Unless you are asked to interject, it's best to be the quiet constant that they know they can turn to if need be.

November—March

You have entered the time to sit and consider all the options. I won't lie, it's a little nerve-wracking to watch how this journey is going to play out. I mean, your child has been playing this sport for years now. This isn't just an extra-curricular activity; this is part of who they are.

Now something that they have worked for, for such an extended period, could open the door to education or other pursuits in a huge way. I also tell parents to take the time to reflect and congratulate your child for making it this far.

Your child might not respond to the affirmation that you are giving to them at that moment. Believe me, as a former athlete, I can tell you that it means so much. It truly does. Don't neglect to give your child that because it will be part of the strength that they draw from when making what amounts to one of the biggest decisions of their young lives.

SECTION THREE
POST SEASON CYCLE OF SUCCESS
THE PINNACLE OF THE PROCESS

If you've made it this far in the process, things are getting hot! When I say hot, I mean that things are moving forward at a feverish pace. What seemed like a daunting journey is now almost dragging you along from one road trip to another. One phone call after another, decision, after decision. Don't forget that you are about to have a high school senior on your hands, if they are not a senior already.

At this point, I have attempted to give you some support and establish more confidence in the recruiting process with stories that I felt would really help you get in touch with the expectations that are going to be out there. Ultimately, I want you to be able to make better decisions and provide emotional support as the parent of a student athlete with a sought-after skill set and love of their sport. Now, I need to get you ready with some information that you can sink your teeth into.

When Recruiting Heats Up

There are Do's and Don'ts of recruiting; I want you to familiarize yourself with some of these basics before the clock starts ticking and the pressure is applied. There are a lot of things that parents don't know, but they should. This goes back to education for yourself and protection for your child.

The Do's and Don'ts

Let's start at the beginning...according to NCAA rules, a school can't contact a potential recruit until *June 15th going into their junior year*. By then if a kid is going to be recruited, they've already been identified by colleges as someone that they will be reaching out to when the time comes.

In my experience with my son, he received his first piece of mail from a university when he was a freshman in high school. I knew then that his scope of work, between AAU and his high school team, had put him on the radar. Receiving letters from schools is a common part of the process; it's a good way to gauge who may be interested in your child.

Let's look at this in phases so that you'll know who's flirting with you; who's asking you out; and who's ready to say I do. When you know what stage the relationship is in, you are better able to identify who to respond to. This will inevitably stop you from wasting time with a wink when someone else is standing there with a ring.

Phase 1. (FLIRTING)

As I stated earlier, receiving letters from schools is a good indicator of which programs may be interested in your child. This means that the school knows about a kid and has identified him or her as a potential recruit. However, it's important to keep everything in perspective because this is just the beginning of the process. You may receive more letters from one school than from others.

At this stage, keep in mind that most of the interest is based on data and generic numbers. The coaches have a file with information on potential recruits like, height/weight, scoring, rankings, etc. If your child fits what they are looking for on paper, they might be contacted for camp invites or recruiting questionnaires. Some larger athletic programs have an initial recruiting list with thousands of potential recruits. Don't get too excited with a little flirting.

I can tell you that many times, the recruiting process starts to shift directions. You could end up growing fond of a school that you, and your child, never expected. Believe me, stranger things have happened.

Phase 2. (ASKING YOU OUT)

On June 15th, going into your child's junior year, things will begin to heat up more. They'll begin to get phone calls and text messages from schools who are interested. You will be able to determine the level of interest in your child based on how many schools are calling, texting, and sending letters to make initial contact with him or her. Pay close attention to this.

In my experience with my son Lorne Jr., I noticed that he was getting a lot of calls from assistant coaches. I didn't understand until later that one of the primary job responsibilities of an assistant coach is to recruit talent. He or she is assigned to do this so that the head coach can evaluate the potential recruit and ultimately make the determination of whether to offer that kid a scholarship or not.

In this phase you'll notice that the assistant coach who is pursuing your child may try to get him to the campus on an unofficial visit. According to NCAA rules, you're allowed to take as many unofficial visits as you want. Keep in mind that an unofficial visit is when you're solely responsible for all of your travel expenses (i.e. plane tickets, hotel rooms, spending money etc.) to get to and from their campus. If a school is asking you to come on unofficial visits this is a good indication that you're on their recruiting board. Your student's name has probably been coming up in recruiting meetings at that school.

Phase 3. (READY TO SAY I DO)

As Lorne Jr's. recruiting continued to heat up, I noticed that the head coaches began getting involved. They started texting and calling him directly and regularly. In the beginning, the assistant coaches were making all the contact with my son; coming to his school during open gym period; and attending his games, etc. Then I noticed a shift in who was contacting him. The head coaches were coming out to see him play themselves to make their own in-person evaluations of his potential and skill level.

I can vividly recall one day Lorne Jr.'s high school coach called me and said, "I just hung up the phone with the head coach of a *major program*. He was asking me a ton of questions about your son. He wanted to know about you, his mom, his brother, and his sister. He asked me what type of kid Lorne was, and he wanted his school transcripts."

I said, "WOW!" The next day the head coach called back and they wanted to come to the school on the following Sunday to see Lorne Jr. play. Because it was a Sunday, Lorne's coach had to arrange a special open gym workout. Just as the workout began, three people walked in -- the head coach, the assistant coach, and the pilot of the private jet they took to fly in to see my son play.

The open gym lasted for two hours. After it was over, they left and flew back home. I didn't know it until later, but it turned out that my son was the only order of business for them that day.

The following day, the head coach texted my son and invited him on an official visit to their campus. An official visit is when the school is very interested in your child and a scholarship offer is very likely. The school pays for everything, including the plane tickets, hotel, food, etc. Although a kid can receive a scholarship offer on an unofficial visit, the chances of an offer are much higher on an official visit.

In November of his junior year, they flew me and my son to their campus on an official visit. They treated us first-class all the way. They picked us up from the airport and immediately took us to their facility where the school's Athletic Director was waiting. He met with us privately to talk about the school and everything it had to offer. After the team practice ended, the head coach took us to his office for a presentation about the program, and what a degree from their university would mean for my son for the rest of his life.

Before he started, he offered my son a full athletic scholarship to attend the university and to play basketball for him and his team. I was blown away by the professionalism and the level of detail in which they approached the recruiting process. It made me realize just how serious recruitment is to the colleges and universities involved.

I'm not saying that every athlete is going to have the same experience that my son had. I'm also not saying that every visit by a college coach will end up in an offer, or that if you receive a letter of interest that it will turn into a signed national *Letter of Intent*.

By no means am I saying that my son was the only choice for the school that he ultimately received his scholarship offer from. I'm humbly saying that as a parent, my child's journey through the recruitment process has shaped me more than I could have ever imagined.

I know that having children, in my case a daughter and two sons, who are talented and determined has made me a better man on so many levels. The joy I get from being their Dad and the responsibility that comes with that title is higher, richer, and more overwhelming than I can express sometimes. I can also tell you that I didn't see athletics being such an enormous part of our lives; not in the way that it has become.

We want our children to be successful at whatever they decide to do. Yes, I'm proud and happy for the scholarship offer, but do you know what really makes the recruitment process worthwhile? It's the fact that my son has been given a financial advantage for his life, and the life of his own family years from now. Whether he decides to continue in sports, or take another path, my child is happy to be attending the University of Wisconsin-Madison.

He thinks the pain, the challenges, the shaping, and the breaking was worth it. Remember no smooth side to the top of the mountain?

Most people would read this and think that this is the end, but they would be wrong. The signed *Letter of Intent* is just the beginning.

Parents, the moment the ink dries is the moment that another season begins; and with it comes a whole new set of challenges, choices, and opportunities that one would never realize could be part of the package. After all, wasn't the scholarship offer to play collegiate sports the goal all along? How could there be more when we reached the goal and finished the journey?

Life is a season of cycles. There will always be another goal, another season, and another cycle that will test your child's character, perseverance, skill set, and heart for not only this game, but for life in general.

All I can tell you is that the journey never truly ends and there is always something to learn, not only for your child, but for you as their parent.

Sports in and of itself is merely a time and place where they will make memories, and touch milestones. Nothing is going to be the same for you or for them after going through the recruitment process.

I hope that reading this book will encourage your heart, help your perspective, and ignite your passion for life, success, and family; all connected by love and covered by faith.

I truly believe that you can and will see a successful outcome for your child, no matter where the path of life might take them. I commend your commitment to help your athlete and be all that God has created them to be. Always remember that it's never over, because each of us is growing from one season to the next. Whether pre, regular, or post, there's always a time to flip the page to the next period of life which is full of possibilities as long as you refuse to never give up!

Until next time, I'll see you in the off-season.

Lorne Sr.

OUR FAMILY
Bowman
TAKING OUR SHOT

BOWMAN
10

ABOUT THE AUTHOR
Lorne Bowman, Sr.

Lorne Bowman, Sr. was born and raised in Detroit, MI; the youngest of 12 children. He resides in Pontiac, MI with his two sons and daughter. Lorne is a poet, songwriter and singer, author, entrepreneur, and a single father. Lorne recognized the extraordinary talent his oldest son had on the basketball court when his son was just four years old. This inspired him to become a basketball trainer so that he could cultivate his son's talents and to be an integral part in his basketball career.

Lorne has devoted his life to raising his children and instilling in them the discipline needed to always strive to reach their full potential. Although challenging at times, Lorne's drive, determination and commitment over the years were rewarded when, through hard work and dedication his son, Lorne, Jr., earned a full four-year basketball scholarship to the University of Wisconsin.

In hopes of helping other parents and their children realize their dreams, Lorne desires to share the successes he has achieved and setbacks he's endured in helping his son excel in basketball. Through his company, Shots Up LLC, Lorne is dedicated to teaching children the importance of creating and maintaining a clean image, as well as expounding on what's necessary for a child to get off to a good start as they pursue their athletic dreams. In addition, Lorne wants to show every parent how vital it is to educate themselves on the ins and outs of the recruiting process.

Notes...

Made in the USA
Columbia, SC
01 March 2021